Herb growing

Violet Stevenson

Pocket Gardener

Sampson Low

Published 1977 by Sampson Low,
Berkshire House, Queen Street, Maidenhead,
Berkshire SL6 1NF
Designed and produced for Sampson Low by
Intercontinental Book Productions

SBN 562 00074 7

Design by Design Practitioners Limited

Photographs supplied by Floraprint Limited (copyright I.G.A.), Leslie Johns and Associates, Harry Smith, DP Press, Suttons Seeds, Marshall Cavendish.

Cover photograph supplied by A-Z Collection.

Printed in Italy

Contents

1 What is a herb?

In spite of its general use in describing a plant which is grown for its scent or flavour, the term 'herb' actually has more than one meaning. Botanically, it is a plant which, unlike a tree, has a stem or stems which die back at the end of its season. Thus, the name 'herb' refers, botanically, to thousands of annual, biennial and perennial plants which are by no means aromatic or wholesome. In the non-botanical sense, herbs are the leafy or soft flowering parts of certain plants. These can be used in the preparation of food or for medicine, for cosmetic purposes, for potpourris, insect repellents and scented toilet waters. Some may even be used in wines and liqueurs.

Spices, often used with herbs in certain dishes, are sometimes confused with them. Spices are not leafy. Usually they are the seeds of a plant. Sometimes, as in the case of the nutmeg, they are the fruit of a tree. Mace, also from the nutmeg tree, is the dried membrane which surrounds the nut when it is growing. Cloves are flower buds, cinnamon is the bark of a tree. Some plants, for instance perennial fennel, provide both spice and herb, but this is not general. It should not be assumed that every part of every culinary herb is good to eat.

The spices used in potpourris are a little more varied and exotic. Orris root is the dried, ground root of the Florentine iris. Angelica root can be dried and used for the same purpose as orris. Calamus is powdered palm root. Khus-khus is fragrant grass. Some plant resins are fragrant. These include gum benzoin and gum olibanum or frankincense. Balsam is an oil-resinous sap tapped from certain trees.

Fennel (above) is an attractive herb to grow in a flowe border and is tall enough to act as a background for ot plants. Fresh parsley (left) can be used as a garnishing as well as lending its own special flavour to a wide variety of dishes.

To carry the distinction even further, culinary herbs are always added to a dish. Except for tisanes or herb teas, they do not form the basis of a dish itself. Thus, while garlic is a herb, onion, a close relative, is a vegetable.

In spite of the true botanical meaning of the term, to most people's minds, herbs are not necessarily plants which die back at the end of the season. Some – the herbaceous kinds – do, but there are also some herbs which are trees, such as the bay, and others which are shrubs, albeit very small ones, such as thyme, sage and rosemary.

Most of the plants we grow as culinary herbs are 'cut-and-come-again' kinds. Fortunately, some of these are evergreens and last for years. These include sage, thyme, rosemary, winter savory and lavender.

The long stem-like leaves of chive (above) have a delicate flavour and, when chopped, are a culinary delight. Sage (left) is used in Italian cuisine. Its purple flowers are ideal in borders.

Constant clipping keeps these plants neat and compact. Although they have a summer flowering season, at which time they are best gathered for drying, they are available all the year round. Obviously, growth is greater in summer, but the leaves are also there to be gathered fresh in mid-winter. Where the climate is cold, these plants can either be grown in a sheltered place or they can be given winter protection. The less exposed they are to the cold, the more shoots they will produce. Some of these evergreen herbs are such handsome plants that they deserve to be grown in some decorative manner, a subject which is discussed in chapter 3.

Most people prefer to have plants which come up year after year; fortunately, there are many herbs which are herbaceous perennials. These include chives, bergamot, tarragon, marjoram, fennel and mint. Usually, the more these are picked the more shoots they will produce. It is often an advantage to keep picking the tips of the stems so that the plant does not flower. For instance, once mint has bloomed, it begins to die down and so from late summer is of little use; yet if the shoot tips are taken as they are ready, more will be produced down the stem, and fresh mint can be picked right on into the autumn. Fennel, a truly handsome plant, can also be

All parts of lovage (top) except the roots have value in cooking. The leaves and stems have a celery-like flavour. The delicate flowers of coriander (above) make a delightful bouquet but it is the seeds that are used in cooking. This particular variety of thyme (right) has a pungent lemon-like scent.

something of a nuisance if it is allowed to drop its seed because seedlings will then sprout up all over the garden. Further, if allowed to flower, the sweet young succulent shoots do not form and only the large, tough leaves are available. If fennel seed is required, it is best to allow just a few stems to seed and to keep taking the young shoots from the others. Once chives have flowered, the plants begin to die down. Where a row of chives is grown as an edging alternate plants could be allowed to flower, while the others are constantly cut, to provide a decorative effect. Like many other perennials, chives are kept rejuvenated if the plants are lifted and divided every three or four years.

The handsome angelica is a biennial, yet if it is prevented from flowering it will come up again the following year, and again the year after that and so on if the same method of removing the flower buds is followed. Otherwise, once it has flowered and set seed it will die.

Parsley is also a biennial, but since we do not cultivate it for its seed, which is produced the year after sowing, it is treated as an annual and therefore sown afresh each year.

There are many annuals among the herbs. Those which are grown for their

Pots of thyme (left) can be grown indoors by a sunny window or on a sheltered terrace. Angelica (middle left) is a giant among herbs. The seeds of caraway (bottom left) are used in bread making. Dill (below) is used as a pickling spice.

leaves should be sown in succession to provide a constant supply.

It is an interesting fact that the main herbs are from just a few plant families. Those which are most versatile and offer the greatest range of flavours come from the parsley family or *Umbelliferae.* The flowers of these plants grow in flat or rounded umbels. Parsley, *Petroselinum crispum,* has a swollen-rooted form known as Hamburg parsley which produces both edible leaves and roots, the latter looking and tasting like small choice parsnips.

Chervil, *Anthriscus cerefolium,* resembles parsley in appearance, but is generally more delicate. It has a slight licorice flavour. It is one of the *fines herbes* and really should be included in every herb garden.

Carrying a similar flavour is sweet cicely or Spanish chervil, *Myrrhis odorata.* Like the Hamburg parsley, its roots can be cooked and its leaves used like chervil or parsley.

Fennel, *Foeniculum vulgare,* comes in two forms. The first is used in the same way as any green herb, as a garnish or in soups and sauces, while the second, *F.vulgare* var.

flowers are attractive as well as excellent examples of this characteristic. Sage, *Salvia officinalis,* is a small shrub. There are other attractive forms of this useful plant that are described more fully on page 22.

Thyme has many species which differ from each other slightly in habit. There are also some variegated forms and varieties. The common thyme most used in cooking is *Thymus vulgaris.* The lemon-scented thyme is *T.*x. *citriodorus.*

Mint also is more varied than is usually realised. There are many species and only a few are cultivated. *Mentha spicata* is the common spearmint. *M. rotundifolia* with more rounded, woolly leaves is known as the apple mint. *M.*x *alopecuroides,* a cross between *M. longifolia* and *M. rotundifolia* is not common but well worth growing if it can be found. Peppermint is *M. piperita.* Pennyroyal is *M. pulegium.* These are the most commonly cultivated mints although there are many more which can also be used. All are perennials.

Fast-growing chervil (left) matures from seed in a mere two months. Apple mint (below) has woolly leaves and dense spikes of pinkish flowers.

dulce, known as sweet or Florence fennel, is a variety with swollen stem bases which form a 'bulb'. It is grown as an annual and used as a salad, much in the same way as celery.

Dill, *Anethum graveolens,* provides both leaves and seeds and is an annual. The same remarks apply to anise, *Pimpinella anisum.* Caraway, *Carum carvi,* a biennial and treated as such, is grown for its seeds alone, as are coriander, *Coriandrum sativum,* and cumin, *Cuminum cyminum.*

Lovage, *Ligusticum officinale,* the last herb in this umbelliferae list, is a hardy perennial. It has a strong characteristic celery flavour, which is the reason its leaves are used in soups and bouillon when celery itself is not available.

The next largest group of herbs is to be found in the sage family or *Labiatae,* the plants with 'lipped' flowers – the sage

Marjoram (left) grows well in a sunny site but does require some winter protection in cold climates.

Rosemary (below left) is a handsome shrub that can be wintered out of doors in a mild climate but elsewhere must be grown as a pot or tub plant that can be moved inside during cold weather.

There are several varieties of mint. One of the most popular for flavouring iced tea is peppermint (below).

While the individual flowers of mints and thymes are very small, forming in a mass a pretty inflorescence all the same, those of the rosemary, *Rosmarinus officinalis,* are larger and differently distributed on the stem. They are an attractive blue and when the plant blooms in late spring, its stems are smothered with these pretty, lipped flowers. The flowers can be used in salads and they can be candied. The plant is a shrub. Only the tips should be picked and this has the effect of keeping the plants neat and bushy. There are many varieties including one with white flowers, and one variety that grows much taller and more erect than the others. Rosemary and its varieties are grown outdoors all year round in mild climates. Elsewhere they are grown in pots or tubs. One variety, *R. humilis* is of low and spreading habit.

Marjoram or origanum comes in several species. *Origanum majorana* is a tender sub-shrub usually treated as a half-hardy annual and known as sweet or knotted marjoram. *O. onites* is the perennial pot marjoram. *O. heracleoticum* is winter marjoram and not quite so hardy as pot marjoram. *O. dictamnus* is Dittany of Crete, and *O. vulgare* is the native European species of which there are other forms to be mentioned later.

Balm (above left) is a hardy perennial that will grow well even in shade. The aromatic leaves are most refreshing in tisanes. Laurel or bay (above) is the only herb to grow to tree size. It is winter-hardy in mild climates. Basil (left) is easy to grow from seed and can be raised both outdoors and indoors in pots and trays.

'Cosmetic and potpourri herbs', page 46.

The Liliaceae or lily family gives us the essential garlic, *Allium sativum*, and the shallot, *A. ascalonicum,* both of which are bulbous plants which are raised annually from 'seed' bulbs or individual cloves in the case of garlic. From this group also come chives or *A. schoenoprasum,* a hardy perennial which is easily grown from seed although plants can also be increased by division.

The splendid bay, *Laurus nobilis*, is the only true laurel, even though there are other, non-edible plants known by this name. It is also the only tree among the

Garlic (left) is a pungent herb that comes in familiar clustered bulb shape, each section of which is called a clove. French tarragon (below) is much more flavourful than the Russian variety. It is widely used in sauces and vinegars.

Two kinds of basil are grown, sweet basil, *Ocimum basilicum,* and bush basil or *O. minimum.* Both are half-hardy annuals and are discussed more fully in the section 'Herbs from seed', page 30.

Balm, sometimes called lemon balm and even lemon mint, is *Melissa officinalis,* a hardy perennial with insignificant lipped flowers. It forms a large dense mass of roots and must be kept under control.

Bergamot, *Monarda didyma,* is the source of Oswego tea and is used mainly for this tisane, although the leaves and flowers are also good in salads. This is a decorative plant and is discussed more fully in 'Colour in the herb garden', page 20.

The daisy family, or *Compositae,* provides us with a few important herbs such as tarragon, *Artemisia dracunculus,* a hardy perennial. French tarragon is a variety with dark green smooth leaves, while Russian tarragon has less smooth leaves which have a milder taste. Other species of artemisia are grown for potpourris and other household uses and are dealt with in

herbs. Its great advantage, apart from its highly individual flavour, is that where it is not possible to let it grow to its full height and width it will still grow well confined in a tub or some other large container. Here it is best constantly trimmed to shape.

There are a few other solitary herbs which may appear to have only little culinary value, yet all the same come into their own on occasions and so are well worth growing. These are discussed more fully later.

2 Herb gardens

Most people imagine a herb garden as a place apart, a special plot set aside for special plants, although not necessarily specially designed. A herb patch is often to be found at the edge of a vegetable patch, down the end of a path, in some odd corner – a horticultural afterthought. Yet no matter how small, a herb garden can be both attractive and interesting.

However, before radically changing an existing garden to accommodate a special herb plot, it is as well to realise that all herbs are basically garden plants. They can be scattered about the garden or grown at different sites, just like any other garden plant. Annuals can go in annual borders or among bedding plants, just as they can be sown in rows among the other vegetables in the kitchen garden. Perennials can go in the herbaceous border; indeed some are grown more for their appearance than for their flavour by some gardeners. The shrubby herbs can be planted in shrub borders or in mixed borders. Some of the sprawling kinds can be introduced into the patio or on to any paved area, where they will revel in the warmth of the sun held by the stones. Some can be grown in tubs and other kinds containers.

So much depends upon how important role the herbs are to play. Obviously, herbs are used daily it is essential maintain a constant and adequate suppl The greater the variety of herbs at one disposal, the less one is likely to depen upon one particular herb, and so it migh be helpful to make changes with this i mind. For instance, where chervil an fennel are grown these can be used in plac of parsley for certain dishes. They can als be mixed with it. If it is decided to grow th herbs among the other garden plants, might be necessary to grow those herb which are most frequently gathered parsley and chives for instance, in som other place – as a vegetable row, or as path edging, for example.

Culinary herbs can be planted in th same bed or border as the cosmetic o fragrant herbs, and where a special herl garden is being designed this has grea advantages. One kind of plant can be usec to separate a group of another kind.

For convenience, it is useful to site a herb

Herb gardens range from tiny corner plots to magnificent formal gardens laid out amid stately paths and set off by elaborately trimmed shrubbery (right).

The massed spikes of flowering thyme and the pretty tufted heads of chive add a delightful splash of colour to an informally arranged herb border (left).

plot near the house although, of course, this is not essential. However, where fresh herbs are preferred to dried ones, even in winter, it is helpful to have them near at hand. Also, a bed near a house is often more protected than one in the open.

A patch of earth as small as 1m (3ft) square should prove adequate for a small family. It is also important in this case to realise that a great many herbs can be grown in containers, which means that the small plot can be extended in an attractive manner. Before deciding which plants to grow in the open soil, it is worth learning which will grow well in containers. There are more details in chapter 5, 'Herbs in limited spaces', page 38. Ideally, the thing to do would be to design a little bed near the house and among paving, so that this could be complemented and supplemented by, for instance, a pair of clipped bays placed one on each side of the doorway, rosemary trained against the house wall, thyme at the very edge of the bed and encouraged to sprawl over the paving, and winter savory in wide, low tubs or giant saucers placed on the paving.

As you would expect, the taller a plant grows the more space it will require at ground level, usually because its lower leaves are so large. This means that tall plants such as angelica are really not suitable for a very small plot. On the other hand, fennel, which is also tall although not so bulky, can be kept fairly well under control simply by gathering it often and keeping the tips of the shoots from flowering.

The few herbs which grow in a small plot

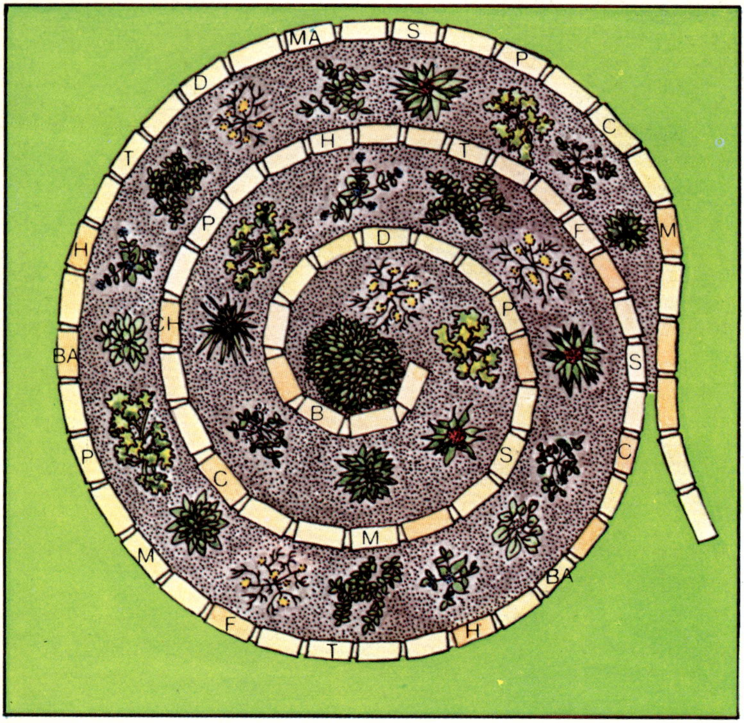

A corner of a small garde
can be transformed into
compact and colourful
herb area by building a
snail garden. From a sho
distance away it will
resemble a small island
set off by the surroundin
lawn. Here, the followin
herbs have been grown
B – bay
BA – basil
C – chervil
CH – chives
D – dill
F –fennel
H – hyssop
M – mint
MA – marjoram
P – parsley
S – sorrel
T – thyme

are likely to be cut often, which is a good thing, for this means that the plants remain neat and compact. This is another reason for increasing the variety of plants grown rather than to grow several of only one kind. These several may not all be cut often enough.

Incidentally, it should be borne in mind that while annual kinds, or those treated as annuals, can be cut as soon as the leaves are large enough, it may take perennials and shrubs two or three years to become established. These should not be cut heavily during the first year; indeed it is best to leave them alone during this time. Later, when at least some of them are large enough to be divided, it is best to lift only one and to leave the other one or two as a supply. When the divided plant is ready for cutting, the other can be lifted and discarded or divided as the case may be.

Some herbs are inclined to dominate the rest, usually because they have invasive roots. Mint is an example. Where a ver small herb plot is being planned, it is best t grow the mint separately in a deep container, preferably in shade or partial shade If this cannot be done, the roots should b isolated in some way.

Fortunately, herbs lend themselves to both formal and informal planting and to both modern and traditional designs of beds and borders. There are some charming traditional patterns which fit well into small modern gardens. For instance, a square or rectangular plot will take a snail-shell herb garden. The 'snail' is made by making a paved path which goes round inside the rectangle in ever decreasing circles until the centre is reached. The soil on each side of the continuous curving path is planted with herbs.

Snail gardens can be very attractive, but success depends upon what herbs are grown and how they are planted. If the plants are very tall and straggly the effect is

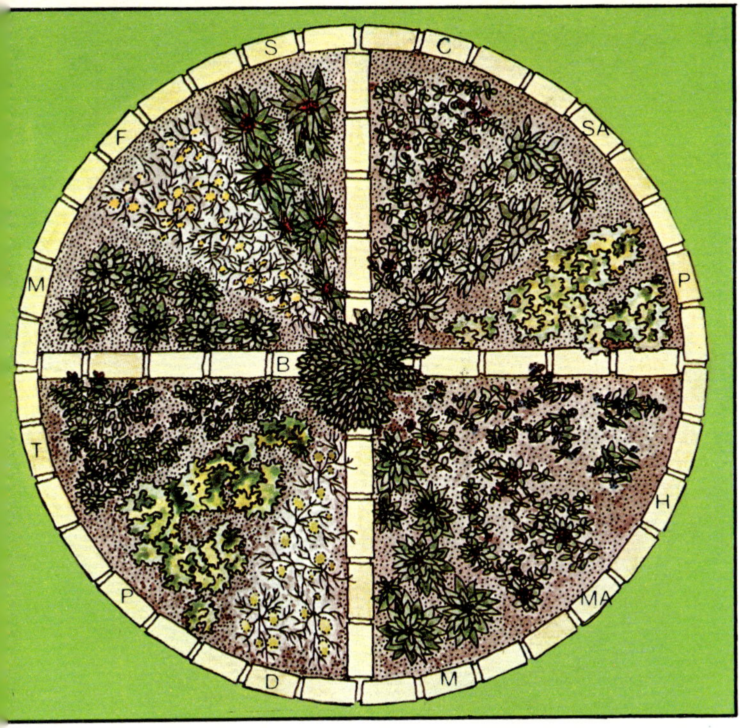

A cartwheel shape is another compact and useful way to grow herbs. Here, a number of different varieties radiate out from an imposing bay tree at the 'hub' of the garden.
B – bay
C – chervil
D – dill
F – fennel
H – hyssop
MA – marjoram
M – mint
P – parsley
S – sage
SO – sorrel
T – thyme

ıst. Tall plants can be grown in the corners ſ the rectangle left by the curving path. hese can be in groups either of one kind or ıixed. The latter will probably be more ttractive, but much will depend upon the rea available. The smallest and most ɔmpact herbs should be planted or sown ose to the edge of the paving so that they ɔllow the lines of the curve. The slightly ıller ones can go behind these. It is best to ork from the shortest plants at the very eginning of the snail path, gradually going pwards, until the centre is reached.

Another favourite is the cartwheel pat- ern, in which a circular plot is divided into vedge-shaped sections radiating out from a entral ring, thus imitating the spokes and ub of a wheel. Usually, a different kind of erb is planted in each section, although he imaginative gardener may devise ttractive bedding schemes, with contrast- ıg colours and textures mingling together ı alternate beds with the plain greens between them. Alternatively, beds can be reserved for the annual kinds, such as parsley and chervil, or for those herbs which are constantly clipped, such as chives.

If the area is large enough the sections should be divided by narrow paths, otherwise they are divided by a band of low-growing herbs, possibly and preferably all of one kind. Paths can be paved, simply trodden down or – and this is more in the spirit of a herb garden – be carpeted with low-growing and spreading herbs such as some varieties of thymes and pennyroyal. Camomile can also be used for this purpose, but this has to be clipped more frequently or it will not form a mat. The other two herbs should be clipped after flowering.

The garden looks better, also, if a path is made round its perimeter. This can be both prettily and usefully edged by a border of those plants which are frequently cut, such as chives, parsley, marjoram and basil, so that these are conveniently placed even in

Even a space as small as a single square metre can b transformed into a herb garden. Try growing thyme (a chives (b), borage (c), parsley (d), marjoram (e), sage (f mint (g), and tarragon (h) in the pattern shown.

very wet weather. These in turn can be alternated with shallots which are attractively spiky and a pleasant bright green while growing. Their fading leaves at the end of summer will be well masked by the herbs. For the little space these plants occupy, the rewards are great.

Where the garden suits its setting, in an old cottage garden for instance, or as part of a garden of a house built two or three centuries ago, a knot garden made after the Elizabethan style can look delightful. In this case, each bed, carefully hedged apart from the other beds, contains just one kind of herb, is geometrically shaped and forms part of an overall pattern. Usually, there i a gravel or shell walk between each bed.

Most of the evergreen herbs stand clip ping; indeed, this is often the only means c keeping some in good condition. Wher culinary herbs and others are grown in th same garden, dwarf lavenders can be use as hedging. Hyssop is also attractive.

Some herbs make good edgings to bed and borders of other kinds of plants, ever rows of vegetables. The side of a vegetabl plot, with the vegetable rows at right angle to it, will be improved in appearance as wel as made more productive if it is plantec with a variety of herbs. Obviously, the talest kinds will have to be thoughtfully placed. Usually, these are best at the ends of the border. A useful border can be made to follow the edge of any garden path. Herbs fill the area both attractively and economically and it is always helpful to have herbs growing where they can be easily reached and cut in wet weather and in winter. Obviously, the shortest, most compact plants are best for this purpose. These include both perennials and annuals, for instance thymes, chives, parsley, savory, basil, marjoram, sage; the latter should be kept short. Some evergreen kinds should be included so that the border is still well defined and attractive in winter.

In a border, the herbs are planted in much the same way as other plants in a herbaceous border. However, it is wise to site the most used in a convenient place. If you have to cross a wide border to reach a

Herbs can be raised in rampant borders (right) or in compact bunches (below) against a warming wall.

Keep lavender neatly shaped (right) by trimming the flowers and rapidly growing young shoots.

A luxuriant bay (left) surrounded by an informal arrangement of rosemary, sage, hyssop and thyme can create a wild but natural look in a suitably large garden.

plant, add a few paving stones to step on.

It is not essential that a wide herb border, as opposed to an edging border, be straight. 'Island' beds can also be used for herbs. In this case, the very tallest plants should go to the centre. In a 'backed' border they should be planted at the back. If plants are too strictly zoned into tall, medium and short, the border can look dull. A better effect is gained if some of the plants of medium height are placed in front.

Fortunately, very few herbs need staking. Dill is an exception. Fairly tall twiggy sticks – pea-sticks – are best for dill. These should be pushed into the ground round the plants while they are young so that they can grow against and through the twigs. They will then be held quite fast and the supports will be hidden. Tall fennel and angelica are usually sturdy enough to stand unaided, but sweet cicely sometimes needs support. Much depends upon the frequency and strength of the prevailing wind.

When planning a mixed border, put the evergreens in place first, leaving plenty of space around them. Most of these are fairly short, which means that they will not smother any of the annual kinds planted between them. If there seems danger of this happening, keep the evergreens frequently clipped. Clippings can always be dried.

Most herbs prefer a well drained soil. This does not need to be specially rich, but it should be light. Heavy soil has an effect upon the pungency of plants. If a plant appears not to be doing as well as it should, it can always be given plant food in a soluble form and this should act as a tonic. Where soil is heavy it can be made lighter by adding humus, peat and some sand.

Most herbs originate in hot, sunny countries, but not all grow best in full sun. Some prefer shade or partial shade, at least in summer. Mint will grow best where the soil is slightly moist and there is some shade. In summer, both chervil and parsley will grow lusher in shade, although chervil will germinate quickly in a sunny warm spot early in the year.

Where the border is sited in a sunny place, shade can often be provided, at least for part of the day, by some taller plant.

Where an island bed is made, or where a border runs from east to west, there is always a shady or shadier side.

A good way to use a herb border is as a link between the utility and decorative sections of a garden. Where the existing soil is neither light nor warm, there is an advantage in making a raised border or a bank. A raised border need be no more than one brick high, or it can be stepped so that one level, wide enough for short herbs, is one brick high, with another level two bricks high above. The bed can be made higher than this if required. This method is particularly effective if you wish to hide the utility garden from the decorative part, because the raised bed holding tall plants higher from the ground acts as a screen in summer. In winter, although the tall plants are cut down, the raised bed provides protection for the vegetable area.

A long mound does not entail so much preliminary labour, and it can be gradually raised as the years go by. Annual mulching with peat, well-rotted manure and compost will keep the plants in good health as the mound increases in height. The soil will certainly be well drained. Many of the herbs will help to bind the banked soil and hold it in place.

This formal herb garden demonstrates the elaborate layout and colour that can be achieved in a well-planned garden.

3 Colour in the herb garden

Many culinary herbs are extremely handsome, with foliage ranging through many hues of green as well as grey, silver, bronze and purple. Some have leaves which are variegated in yellow, cream or white, and some have multi-coloured variegation. When these plants flower, they add colour and beauty to the garden. Some have lacy umbels of white; others have thick yellow umbrella-like flowers borne aloft on tall stems. There are leafy stems studded with lipped flowers of rose red and carmine. There are fascinating whorls, tufts and spikes of these same colours as well as blue, violet and soft mauves.

All this means that a herb garden can be decorative, an important point where the main garden is small and there are no far corners in which the less flamboyant plants can be hidden away. However, the herb garden can be made even more colourful, for apart from those herbs used mainly for their leaves, there are a few others whose flowers and seeds are also edible. These plants are colourful and pretty and because they are annuals are easily grown. They are borage, pot marigold, *Papaver somniferum,* the dusky mauve, grey-leaved poppy whose seeds are used to garnish bread, and the bright nasturtium. Marigolds and nasturtiums grow well in containers, so where there is not much space in the actual herb bed or border, these can often be grown in raised pots of some kind and placed near the other herbs.

To these herbs roses can always be added, not simply as the odd isolated bush, but also as a hedge or screen.

If potpourri plants are to be included, then the herb plot can be as colourful as any herbaceous border at certain times of the year. Lavender makes a wonderful mass of colour and the flowers last for many weeks. The evergreen, or rather ever-grey, plants remain decorative throughout the year, becoming smudged with the flower colour a few weeks before the flowers actually open and continuing to be pretty in a quiet way as they fade.

Apart from its self colour, lavender *(Lavandula officinalis)* varies. There are some varieties with deep violet flowers, *Lavandula* 'Munstead Dwarf', a popular example that grows about 45cm (18in) tall. There is a white dwarf variety, and a soft and pretty pink-flowered variety. If these are not to be found in a local nurseryman's list or at a garden centre, they are sometimes offered by mail-order specialists. It is always well worth keeping an eye open for them, especially for those which seem to vary even a little more from the usual.

Fortunately, lavender, like most of the other shrubby herbs, is easily propagated by cuttings. Take unflowered shoots from the old wood of a plant. Pull each shoot downwards so that it comes away with a little tail of the skin of the wood. This is known as a 'heel'. It is usual when taking cuttings to trim the heel, but lavender cuttings should be handled as little as possible, so do not trim the heel in this case. Prepare a little good soil in a frame or in some protected place in the open garden; a cloche can be used if necessary. Top the soil with a little clean horticultural sand, water it and make a little hole to take about one-third the length of each cutting. Put them 5–7cm (2–3in) apart, and firm the cuttings in well by treading the soil against them. Water the cuttings once more and leave them to root.

The cuttings should be taken in late summer or autumn. If they are taken in summer, they should go into frames or under cloches. The older the wood from which the shoots are taken, the colder should the cuttings be grown. So it follows that if the cuttings are not taken until the autumn, they have been taken from older wood, and in this case they are best taken and inserted into the open ground in some

A banked herb border can be used as a dividing wall to separate one section of a garden from another.

sheltered place.

It is possible to raise some types of lavender from seed but not all seedsmen carry stocks.

Like lavender, hyssop, *Hyssopus officinalis*, has also given rise to varieties. The species has lipped flowers of a fine rich violet blue. The varieties have white, pink and purple blooms.

This plant, but not the varieties, can be raised from seed. It and the varieties can also be propagated by cuttings, which should be taken in April or May and placed outdoors in some shady spot. The plants can also be divided in spring or in autumn.

One of the mints whose leaves are used in the preparation of potpourris – although also delicious in salads, they are infrequently used this way – is a particularly attractive variegated plant, *Mentha rotundifolia variegata*. The broad, slightly hairy leaves are splashed with creamy-white and when the shoots are young there may be no trace of green on them at all. Sometimes these shoots are a beautiful, delicate tint of magenta.

A hardy geranium or crane's-bill, *Geranium macrorrhizum*, has strongly scented roots and leaves, both of which are used. Apart from this it is a fine garden plant and a splendid ground cover. Its large, attractively shaped leaves soon cover a wide area if required and they turn beautiful colours as autumn approaches. The flowers are borne well above the leaves and are a dusky rose colour.

This plant is a perennial and is very easily propagated by division.

Bergamot, *Monarda didyma*, already referred to as being the herb from which Oswego tea is prepared, has attractive flowers which grow in whorls and are a pleasant dusky rose hue. There are now many cultivars, varieties of this plant whose flowers are in other colours ranging from soft pink to purple – useful if one is planning a full range of colours in a herb border.

For the full impact of colour, it is important to group and site the plants carefully. For instance, both the green-leaved and the

The rose pink colours of flowering bergamot can be used to lend a splash of colour to a herb border.

handsome bronze-leaved varieties of fennel grow between 120–180cm (4–6ft) tall, so it follows that they will look best at the back of a border. Usually, when an ordinary herbaceous border is being made, the gardener is recommended to plant in groups of three so that they make a greater impact, but it is not necessary to follow this rule – nor might it be practical – when planning a herb plot or garden. Fennel is a very well furnished plant and after the first year, soil and other conditions being suitable, it will grow rapidly and fill a space some 60cm (2ft) square. However, fennel is not winter hardy in most northern regions and so is treated as an annual.

As it grows taller and comes into flower the base of the plant becomes slightly bare as the first leaves fade. For this reason it is best to plant some dense-growing plant, possibly an evergreen, in front of it. One of the best plants for this purpose is sage. The grey-leaved common sage is quite handsome, but handsomer by far is the so-called red or purple sage. The new shoots are a rich red-purple. The leaves can be used for cooking in exactly the same way as the common sage.

Another charming umbellifer, though much shorter, about 35–45cm (14–18in), is the pretty coriander. Its flowers, which grow in loose, lacy umbels, are soft lavender-mauve. It needs to be grown near the front of the border, and looks good flanked by the variegated 'silver' thymes. These come into flower a little earlier than the coriander, but the flower heads are retained, misty-mauve, for some time.

Thymes make lovely mats of colour and since all are pungent and can be used, one could supplement the common thyme with others. These are discussed more fully in the following chapters.

It is well worth studying seed catalogues in the hopes of finding unusual herbs. Quite recently the seedsmen introduced a handsome form of basil with dark bronze leaves which are just as pungent as the green. Known as 'Dark Opal', it brings a rare colour to the border – imagine leaves the colour of copper beech.

It is best to raise the plants in boxes and to plant them out at the beginning of summer. They need careful watching over for the first two weeks or so, and watering. Beware of slugs, which seem to like this variety above all others.

To see this plant at its best, grow it next to or near the golden-leaved marjoram. This is an ideal plant to grow right at the edge of a bed or border if it is flanked by a paved path, because the stems will trail over it and soften the edges attractively. The plant is best increased by division in spring or autumn.

The apple-green balm also sports a variegated form whose leaves are blotched with a bright yellow. The colours and their variegation are stronger when the shoots are young, and at this time they are very vivid indeed. Like the green form, this plant is invasive and should be kept under control. The best way of doing this is to lift the entire plant when it has occupied its given space, then to chop off a good portion from the whole mass, using a spade. Enrich the soil a little from which the plant was taken and replant the piece. Do this in spring or autumn.

Chives have pretty little rosy-purple pompom flowers borne on slim stems which take the flowers above the leaves. The flowers can be used in salads. The only drawback to allowing the plants to bloom is that once this happens they begin to die down. If they do not flower, the 'grass'

Bronze fennel is a variety with burnished foliage and makes an excellent foil to the predominant green of a herb garden.

continues to grow. For this reason, flower buds are usually picked off. If the flowers are wanted for colour, it is best to grow plenty of plants and to remove the flowers from some and not others.

The tall, graceful poppy, *Papaver somniferum,* mentioned earlier, has beautiful glaucous leaves, stems, buds and seed capsules and grows to 70–85cm (2½–3ft). Altogether it is a very handsome plant. As one would expect, the foliage and the rest harmonise delightfully with the dusky mauve, sometimes dusky pink, flowers. Fortunately, they also harmonise beautifully with many herbs, especially those with silver, grey or purple in their foliage.

This poppy is easily grown from seed. It will also seed itself. There are 20,000 to 30,000 seeds in each capsule. It is these rich oily seeds which are used in cooking, in bread, confectionery and some desserts. The plants grow best if they are given plenty of space and it is well worth while thinning out seedlings to leave roughly a space from 30–50cm (1–2ft) square for each plant. One plant treated this way will give a better show and very much larger flowers than a mass of inferior plants. This goes for most annuals, incidentally.

The quality of the seeds of the species and the beautiful cultivars seems not to differ and can be used in just the same way. There are lovely double-flowered varieties which are listed in the seed catalogues as 'Peony' or 'Carnation-flowered'. They vary a little in colour from the species, having a slightly wider range. They will also seed themselves, but if they are allowed to do this, after a time they will revert to the species and all will be single-flowered.

Sow the seed of the species or the var-
ieties in September if you want the plants to bloom early, i.e. late spring the following year. Sow the seed in early spring for summer flowering. Like most hardy annuals, this poppy's season is short and so, to ensure a long period of bloom, it is best to make the two sowings. The seed is viable and so long as the opened packet is not kept in an airtight container – although it should be kept out of the way of mice – the seed bought for autumn sowing should keep for the spring and *vice versa*.

Try grouping this poppy next to bronze-leaved fennel with purple and grey sage before it. Try it behind the soft feathery foliage of *Artemisia abrotanum*, southernwood or lad's love. Mild-climate gardeners who have a rosemary hedge, can sow a row of these poppies parallel with it, but should keep a good distance between them because the lush poppies soon smother plants which are too close to them.

A cluster of tall, stately poppies (left) is a colourful and unusual addition to a herb garden. The seeds of this plant are delicious when baked in confectionery. Silvery cotton lavender (right) erupts into brilliant yellow flower balls. Ranked growths of lavender and looming fennel (below) form a wall of contrasting colours.

For those who enjoy a vivid display of floral colour, pot marigolds, poppies and nasturtiums – simple, bright annuals – can be used here and there among the more permanent plants. Alternatively they can be sown in rows in an edging mixture.

Special effects can be achieved by allowing herbs to play special roles. Some herbs are ideal for hedges and often one needs only a low boundary hedge to separate one part of a garden from another – perhaps to limit the area in which herbs are cultivated. Lavender, rosemary (where hardy) and santolina are the best but in climates which are colder germander, *Teucrium chamaedrys*, is a safer choice if the hedge need not be too tall. Germander, which takes well to clipping, will grow about 30cm (12in) high.

Santolina chamaecyparissus, lavender cot-

tons, used as a potpourri component, is an attractive, light silver plant which looks well in association with stone. It softens the edge of a paved area particularly prettily. All santolina hedges as well as those of other plants should be clipped back immediately after flowering to keep them compact. Some gardeners do not allow them to flower but aim to keep them as silver as possible all the time. When they bloom, the flowers are yellow.

The common rosemary's erect form, already described, is the best hedging variety, but any rosemary except the sprawling type will do for this purpose. This, incidentally, is a fine plant for seaside gardens but it cannot safely be recommended for most northern gardens because it is not reliably winter hardy in a colder climate.

Earlier reference was made to the invasive nature of mints and balm. These must be thinned out rigorously or planted in separate bottomless containers if they are grown with other plants to prevent the roots wandering over the soil surface. On the other hand, this particular invasiveness can be used to advantage, for these plants will cover a bank and hold the soil in place. If the plain green forms are used they will be neat rather than decorative, but there

Bottomless pots (above) can be used in the garden to restrain the growth of mint plants. They keep the roo mass within a closely confined space and stop it from spreading rampantly.The flowers of camomile (below form attractive daisy-like heads. When dried they are used to make an extremely refreshing tea.

Spearmint (right) has pointed spearhead-like leaves and purplish flowers that appear in autumn. This is the best known variety of all the mints and is widely used in sauces.

Camomile lawns (below right) are soft and fragrant. They are formed by keeping the creeping stems of the plant cut short but allowing them to spread out and form a living carpet.

are sufficient varieties of these plants which are variegated or coloured in some way to make a covered bank quite interesting. The bergamot mint, *Mentha citrata,* becomes beautifully coloured at the end of summer before it dies down and, of course, a certain amount of colour will be provided by the mint's flowers.

Some mints, the little pennyroyal in particular, can be used to carpet the ground, like the creeping thymes. These plants are tough enough to take a certain amount of walking upon. Camomile also can be used as a lawn, just as it can be used to carpet a path. It has to be clipped or mown occasionally, unlike the mint or thyme. It can also be mixed with grass, in which case it makes a really hardy lawn.

Finally, one should not forget the roses. If potpourri is to be made, then some of the highly scented old-fashioned varieties and

species are essential. Further, these ar culinary plants, once highly regarded as source of health-giving salads, or for speci jams and preserves and wines and vinegars This being the case, they will not look out c place in a herb garden where there is ade quate room to display them. Indeed, the make a delightful backing for a non-islan

Common thyme (left) grows to form a low bush-like shape. It spreads rapidly and, when flowering, become covered in a mass of strong scented tiny purple petals

A border pf Pink Parfait roses and lanky growing laven der (right) forms a beautiful wall of colour when in flower. This particular variety of rose has a deliciousl fragrant scent.

A highly productive and colourful herb garden (below can be established even in a limited space, provided it is a sunny, well-drained location.

border. Roses also look well combined with lavender, and, for a vivid effect, dwarf varieties can be grown alongside them.

How they are grown will depend upon what space is available. Roses can be grown among other plants, but they should not be so crowded that they are smothered. It should be a simple matter to ensure that low plants, such as thyme, grow at their feet rather than tall kinds, such as fennel. However, there are some roses which can be grown as a formal hedge, such as the species *Rosa eglanteria,* the sweet briar. This is an ideal herb garden rose because it has fragrant foliage. It will grow to 180cm (72in) unless trimmed each spring so that it remains compact and under control. The clippings, which are scented, of course, can be dried and used in potpourri.

Do not expect the same long period of flowering from species and varieties of old-fashioned roses generally as from the modern varieties. Most bloom only once, in early summer. Some are followed by decorative fruits, some of which are worth preserving as syrups or as jam; some can be dried and the largest can be cooked like any other fruit in pies.

4 Herbs from seed

Some herbs must be grown from seed. Others can be but it might not prove practical to do so. Annuals and biennials, many of which are sown where they are to mature, grow quickly and are soon ready for cutting, but perennials take much longer. It may be as long as three years from the time that the seed was sown to the time that the plants have made sufficient growth to be cut. This being the case, it is often best to begin with a selection of mature plants. Most nurserymen sell a basic collection and there are also specialist herb growers. Obviously, the larger the plants, the better. If these are canister-grown, they can be bought and planted a any time of the year when the soil is suita ble. Planting should not be carried ou when the soil is frozen. Drought is not great drawback. Water the plants well i the canister an hour or so before plantin and again when they have been taken out the canister and planted in the grounc Keep an eye on them and keep the so round them moist.

Seed is so cheap that it may be though that this is an expensive way of stocking th garden, but it could well prove to be mor economical in the long run. A compromis can be reached which may be helpful fc

Annual herbs such as chervil, dill, borage, and summe savory (left) are quick-growing and can be cut for use within weeks of being planted. Where herbs are frequently used, grow them in convenient rows (right).

those who budget carefully. Just one mature plant of each herb can be bought a a beginning. While this is becoming established and ready for cutting, more of th same kind can be raised from seed gradually filling the border as they come along.

Where a large quantity of certain herbs i to be used, it is often more convenient t grow them in rows like vegetables. Mos herbs treated this way are annuals, wit some biennials such as chervil, basil, summer savory, sweet marjoram, parsley, shallots and garlic. Plants grown for spices - anise, caraway, coriander, cumin and dill - can also be raised this way.

Some of these, chervil for example should be sown where they are to mature simply because they will not transplan well. Most of the others are best sown in boxes or in short nursery rows and lifted and transplanted when they are large enough to handle. This method is usually safer, in as much as the young plants, individually spaced, are not so likely to be eaten by insect pests or slugs; nor are they so

ikely to be influenced by bad weather or by lrought. Also, germination is usually bet-:er when planted this way.

In countries where there is a short sea-ɪon, there is much to be gained by sowing the more tender kinds, and those which will transplant, indoors under fluorescent lights or in a sunny window in the early part of the year. The seedlings germinate very quickly and grow apace. As soon as these are large enough to handle they can be 'pricked off', a term which means lifted, separated and transplanted – either spaced out about 5cm (2in) in boxes, or, better still, into small individual pots. Pot plants are best because they suffer little check when they are transplanted and they are not so liable to become starved while they are awaiting planting outdoors. Usually these little plants are kept indoors until the weather is good. They are then introduced to it slowly, a process known as 'hardening off', by being stood outdoors on good days and brought in at night, or by being transferred to a garden frame or placed under a cloche. When all fear of frost is gone, by which time

they should be well acclimatised to outdoors, they can be planted in their permanent places – permanent, that is, for that year.

Plants usually treated this way include summer savory, sweet marjoram, and basil, both green and ornamental.

It is also possible to steal a march on time and to raise a few kinds of herbs from seed sown in pots and grown on a sunny windowsill or in a greenhouse. These are cut while they are quite young, the plants then being considered expendable. Details are given in chapter 6.

Some seed, especially from certain plants of the umbelliferae, is not long-lived. If a packet has been stored unopened for some months under the wrong conditions, the seed might never germinate. Indeed, once a herb garden has been established, it is a good plan to allow just a few kinds, those with the least viable seeds, to seed themselves. These are chervil, parsley an angelica.

On the other hand, chervil and parsle are often sown in succession so that a co tinuous supply is available, which mean that one cannot wait for the self-sow plants alone. Self-sown chervil is ready onl in early spring. Again, a compromise work best; let some plants seed themselves bu sow more from time to time.

Parsley is notoriously slow in its germi nation, sometimes taking as long as si weeks. Although it is usually sown where i is to mature and then thinned out to giv the plants adequate space, it is ofte quicker and more convenient to sow th seed in boxes and to transplant from these

When seed has to be sown in straigh rows it is simple to draw a shallow dril using a garden line as a guide. Generall speaking, a drill should be as deep as twic the depth of the seeds that go in it. Sow th eed as thinly as possible. If the seeds are to e sown in spaces among existing plants, it elps to define the area in which the plants re to grow. Press a large upturned flower ot on to the raked soil. Sow the seeds hinly in the circular drill thus made. Always cover the drill with soil and always read the soil down lightly to prevent it and he seeds from being blown away by the vind or washed out by the rain.

Even when you sow thinly it will still be ecessary to thin out the seedlings to give ach little plant its own living space. It is est to make two or three thinnings rather

Prick out young herbs (left) when they are large enough o handle, being careful to grasp them by the stem and ot the delicate leaves.

Summer savory (right) is a small bushy annual somewhat like a long-leaved form of thyme.

Miniature herb gardens can be created in trays (below) f the soil is deep enough to protect the roots.

The outer flowers of calendula or pot marigold (left) an not the leaves are used in cooking. Of the two varieties of tarragon, the French (above) has the best flavour. I grows to a spindly mature height of 1 metre (2–3ft).

than to take away the plants in one go. Should disaster strike, there will still be some plants to carry on. Thin out after a shower, or after watering the rows an hour or so beforehand.

Remember, it is not always possible to buy seeds of all herbs. Many plants are propagated by cuttings or by division. Here is a list of the most common herbs which can be raised from seed. Plants grown for their seeds (spices) are also included.

Angelica archangelica, **angelica** Sow packeted seed in March, in deep moist soil in a shady place. Alternatively – and this is likely to be more successful – sow seed when ripe, as soon as it is taken from the plant, in August or September.

Allium schoenoprasum, **chives** Sow seed in boxes in March or April; prick off an transplant outdoors in May. Alternatively sow thinly in pots and begin cutting th 'grass' when seedlings are large enough.

Anthemis nobilis, **camomile** Sow seed outdoors in shallow drills in April where th plants are to flower.

Anthriscus cerefolium, **chervil** Sow at intervals from February to October for succession in boxes, under cloches, in frames or ir the open ground according to the time o the year. Crop matures in 6–8 weeks.

Artemisia dracunculus, **tarragon** Seed can be sown in spring but it is much more usual – and faster – to buy plants.

Borago officinalis, **borage** Sow seed where the plants are to flower, in March for summer flowers, in September for May flowers.

alendula officinalis, **pot marigold** Sow :eds where the plants are to flower in Iarch or April.

arum carvi, **caraway** Best sown as soon as pe in the autumn. Autumn-sown plants ower the following summer. Plants from acketed seed sown in spring do not flower ntil the summer of the following year.

oriandrum sativum, **coriander** Sow seeds in nallow drills, 0.5cm (¼in) deep, 30cm 12in) apart in April in rich, light soil where ıe plants are to flower.

uminum cyminum, **cumin** Sow seeds in shal- ow drills, in May, where the plants are to ower.

oeniculum vulgare, **fennel** Sow outdoors in nallow drills in March, transplant when ıe seedlings are large enough to handle in rdinary soil in a sunny position.

Ielissa officinalis, **balm** Sow seeds indoors ı May. Plant out when seedlings are –10cm (3–4in) high in ordinary soil in a arm sunny place. Or buy young plants.

Ionarda didyma, **bergamot** Sow seed in oxes in March. Keep in cold frame or reenhouse. Plant outdoors in late May.

Iyrrhis odorata, **sweet cicely** Sow seeds in hallow drills in ordinary soil outdoors in April or September. The latter time with ewly ripened seeds gives best results.

Ocimum basilicum, **sweet basil** Sow seed ndoors from March to April. Plant out- loors in late May or early June.

Ocimum minimum, **bush basil** As above.

Origanum majorana, **sweet or knotted mar- oram** Sow seed indoors in March; plant outdoors in April in rich soil in a sunny place. Or buy plants.

Origanum onites, **pot marjoram** Sow seed outdoors in March or April in ordinary soil n a sunny position.

Petroselinum crispum, **parsley** Sow in Feb- uary under cloches or indoors in boxes for early crop, outdoors in shallow drills. Sow n April or May for summer crop, in July to August for late autumn crop, in ordinary out non-acid soil in a sunny position.

Peucedanum graveolens, **dill** Sow in shallow drills, in rich, ordinary soil, in a sunny, open position in spring where the plants are to grow and flower.

Pimpinella anisum, **anise** Sow seeds in shal- low drills in well drained, ordinary soil, in spring where the plants are to flower.

Salvia officinalis, **sage** Sow seed indoors in March in boxes. Plant outdoors in May or June in rich but light ordinary soil in a sunny position.

Sanguisorba minor, **salad burnet** Sow seed in boxes indoors in February to March; plant outdoors in April or May in light but moist ordinary soil in sun or light shade.

Satureia hortensis, **summer savory** Sow seed in shallow drills in ordinary soil in a sunny place in April where the plants are to

Borage is a hardy annual that thrives even in poor soil. Its leaves are used fresh to make infusions.

flower. Alternatively, sow indoors in boxes and transplant later.

Once the perennial herbs are well grown, most can be divided should you wish to increase their numbers. Chives grow better if, once they are three years old, they are lifted and divided each spring. Do this when the plants show above ground again. Some of the surplus divisions can be potted for forcing the following spring.

Shallots and garlic are grown from small bulbs known as 'seed', which in fact they

The little golden bulbs of shallots (right) have a milder flavour than onions and are widely used for pickling. Parsley and chervil (below) can be grown in pots along a sunny window ledge. As these are frequently used herbs, growing several pots at once is a good idea.

are not. One small clove of garlic will grow into a tight cluster of several large bulbs. Once you have harvested a good crop of garlic you can save your own seed. Garlic 'seed' is usually bought from the seed merchant, but that sold for cooking can also be used. So can any cloves which begin sprouting in the kitchen, even though it may not seem the correct season for this.

Plant garlic 5cm (2in) deep and 10–14cm (4–6in) apart any time from late winter to early summer. Lift the bulbs when the tall green tops have faded. First spread them out on the ground to let them dry in the air a

Salad burnet (above) is a perennial whose leaves have a delightful cucumber flavour. White-flowered sweet cicely and woolly-leaved apple mint (below right) are all plants that look attractive growing at the back of a herb border.

little, and then hang them to finish drying in a cool, dry place, by their fading tops. Later they can be made into ropes or simply stored in net bags.

Shallots should be planted 14cm (6in) apart but not deeply. Some people simply push the bulb into the soil, but the trouble with this method is that because the bulb is not firmly anchored it is moved out of position during the night by foraging earth worms. It is best to make a small depression in the soil with a trowel and bury the bulb up to its 'nose' in the earth. Once it begins to grow roots it will pull itself upwards. Wait until all the leaves die right down before lifting the bulbs for storing, unless, of course, using them fresh, which can be done throughout the summer. The green tops can be used like chives or cooked in soups.

To harvest the shallots, first lift the clutch of bulbs with a fork and so allow any remaining roots to dry in the air. Spread them out in the sun for a while. If the weather is moist, spread them out under a cloche or in some dry airy place. When the skins rustle and the bulbs are dry, they can be made into ropes or hung in net bags.

Bulbs can be set aside for seed. If there are any very small bulbs, too small for pickling or cooking, set these aside and plant them in early winter. They will provide good-sized fresh shallots for the following summer.

Formerly, the traditional method was to plant shallots on the shortest day and to harvest them on the longest. Certainly they are very hardy and with garlic are among the first which can be planted in a vegetable patch. However, this is not a rule to be strictly observed. Bulbs can be planted, so long as they are obtainable, until late May or early June. Usually, sound bulbs will last from one season to another.

Some gardeners save some of the newly lifted garlic bulbs and plant the bulbs in autumn, for early crops the following year.

5 Herbs in limited spaces

Where open garden space is limited, it is possible to grow herbs on patios and in containers of all kinds. These need not look strictly utilitarian. Properly planned and grown in good soil, they can be quite attractive, and since many of the best plants for containers are also evergreen these captive gardens can be of interest, and use, the year round.

The possibility of standing a bay tree or two by the door has already been mentioned; indeed, these are ideal plants. If there is room, the bay trees can be accompanied by shrubs such as rosemary, winter savory, sage, thyme and perennial marjoram, either planted in their own containers or growing in company. It is importan of course, to begin with good plants if it hoped to cut herb snippets from them soo after planting. It is also important to realis that the containers should be emptied fro time to time, say every two or three year and replanted. Usually, the existing plant can be divided. Parts not used can be pot ted and used while the larger ones ar recovering and growing. In cold climate the bays must be tubbed so they can b moved inside in winter.

It is easy to become over-romantic abou growing herbs and to forget that one i likely to take all the leaves from one plan say parsley or chives, for just one dish. I

Annual and perennial herbs may be raised in dense clusters in windo boxes (right) provided only that the soil is dee enough to retain moistur and keep the roots from becoming parched in th hot sun.

Where climates are not suitable for herbs to be grown outdoors all year round, they can be raised in containers and tubs (left) that are moved indoors or to more sheltered locations during cold weather. Such compact herb gardens are also ideal for limited spaces. Here, chives, parsley, thyme, basil and marjoram are being grown with a selection of colourful lilies.

follows that unless there are more plants to take the shorn one's place, the cook will have to wait a very long time for her next supply. For this reason, it is important to think in terms of growing more than one plant of most herbs and, so far as herbs raised from seed are concerned, to think of growing several pots of each kind – a container row in fact. These can be grown outside for part of the time, and for part of the year brought indoors to mature on a sunny windowsill. Among these fast-growing herbs are chives, chervil, parsley, basil and mint, the later being increased by roots, not seed. Even though these are annuals or treated as such, and are therefore short-lived, usually they can be cut quite severely and then nursed a while, that is, fed with a little liquid plant food and grown outdoors where they will begin shooting up again. Meanwhile other plants which are fuller, will be taking their place.

As always, much depends upon the space available, but it is often possible to erect some shelves on which pots can stand while they are holding seeds and seedlings. They need to be in good light when they have germinated, otherwise the plants become drawn and of little value. Herbs grow well under fluorescent lights at all stages of growth.

It is not necessary to use large pots for these successional sowings. Pots with roughly 0.5 litre (1pt) capacity will do, although, as one would expect, the larger the pot, the better a plant usually does. What is most important is that the soil should be good. It is possible to buy specially mixed soils, confusingly called composts, which have been scientifically designed for seed sowing and for transplanted seedlings – for the latter they are known as potting soils. Seedlings need a slightly different food than older plants and

Pot-grown herbs (top) can be raised in a thin layer of seed compost over a coarser potting compost. Seeds must be sparsely sown then thinned out to give the young plants space (above). Parsley and mixed herbs (right) can be grown in terracotta 'strawberry pots'.

they do not need it quite so rich, which is why there is a difference in most soil mixtures. However, those mixtures which are known as 'soilless' are sometimes suitable for all purposes, so one should read carefully the descriptions on the wrappings.

It is possible to use the same soil in the pot after the old plant has been removed, so long as this has not been diseased in any way. Where this is done, the old soil should be topped with new, and the plant should also be fed with a soluble plant food once it is growing well.

To save time and space, it is also possible to fill a pot almost to the top with plant soil mixture and then to add a shallow top layer of seed soil mixture. This means that seed can be sown thinly in the top layer. The seedlings need not be transplanted although they are almost certain to need thinning out. Their roots will grow down into the richer soil when they need it. Usually, with the quick-growing herbs, allow three to five plants in each 7cm (5in) pot.

Do remember that contained plants of all kinds need water, and in hot, dry weather, they may need watering two or three times a day. Usually, the smaller the pot, the more likely it is to dry out quickly, even disastrously – because sometimes it is not possible to revive a plant which has become dehydrated. If the surface soil is damp to the touch, the plants' roots are probably moist enough. A pot in which the soil is too dry will give an empty ringing sound when rapped. One way to prevent too rapid loss of water is to plunge each pot up to its rim in a bed of peat which is kept constantly moist, though not sodden. Rows of pots can be plunged in troughs or boxes. As you would expect, pots in shade do not dry out so quickly as those in the sun, but not all herbs like deep shade.

Parsley is a herb which seems in demand and, fortunately, it is very easy to grow this plant in a variety of ways. It can, for instance, be grown in one of the specially designed terra-cotta pots known as 'strawberry' or 'crocus' pots which have pockets set all over the surface. These have one disadvantage, in that the water, poured in at the top, courses down and out through every hole, which means that the soil at the core does not get properly soaked. Once the plants grow well they block the holes and the water loss is not so great. It is best, in the early days, to stand the jar in a low bowl or deep saucer and to keep this filled with water when the weather conditions are dry. When the water no longer courses out of the holes immediately, the pot can be taken from the saucer and stood on its own, when it should be watered from the top.

Parsley also grows well in a hanging basket. Line this with moss, plant the parsley by pushing the seedlings through the moss from the outside of the basket. Begin at the bottom of the basket and cover the parsley roots as you go. Once the lower portion is planted, stand the basket in an empty bucket while the upper sides and the top area are planted. Water the plants carefully. Hang the basket in partial shade and be sure to water it regularly.

Light plastic troughs (above) are ideal for raising miniature gardens in the kitchen. Even hanging baskets can be pressed into service as herb gardens. Below, a parsley basket is shown.

Individual paving stones can be lifted from a terrace or patio and the space used to raise herbs. Here, a gangly fennel plant basks in the reflected warmth of the sun-heated concrete tiles.

Constant watering, which is so essential for most contained plants, tends to leach out the soluble plant foods from the soil, and when this happens plants will become starved and spindly. For this reason it is wise to feed plants regularly with a soluble plant food.

It is possible to raise a good supply of herbs in window boxes and tubs so long as the soil is rich and is kept well watered and fed. As we have seen, some herbs prefer sun and some shade, so this should be taken into account when planning what herbs are to be grown and where. Window boxes need to be fairly deep – not less than 15cm (6in), but deeper if possible.

Where a paved patio or backyard exists, it is sometimes possible to lift an occasional paving stone and to make this area into a tiny herb patch. Where it is possible to lift more than one stone, try to make this appear planned rather than haphazard. Three linked stones might look better than three isolated ones. On the other hand, it might be best to lift a stone from each of the four corners, or in such a way that you leave a square or a diamond-shaped bed in the centre. If there is a shady corner, this could take a large and handsome angelica or a stand of feathery fennel.

One good way of making the most of a little space is to build a raised wall along one or more sides of a yard or patio, two or three bricks high. This, like the area from which a paving stone is lifted, should be filled with good soil. Thyme (or rosemary in mild climates) could be trained to cover some areas of the wall. This would look well alternated with any other good climbing plant such as roses or nasturtiums.

6 Herbs in winter

There is no doubt that fresh herbs are best and are certainly more versatile. It is possible to flavour dishes with dried herbs, and later on we discuss ways of drying, but these are not really suitable for mixing in salads or for garnishing. Part of the herb's value is its visual appeal – and fresh green leaves, no matter how finely chopped, always look better than dried flakes or powder. Of course, herb-flavoured vinegars help to impart herb flavours to salad dressings, but ideally one needs fresh green herbs the year through. Fortunately, there are some which will provide leaves in winter. Naturally, supplies depend upon the weather or the season and on the district or locality in which the garden is situated. In a mild season or in an area where severe frosts are rare, it should be possible to gather fresh herbs of some kind or other right through from the end of summer to spring when larger supplies again become available.

In some cases it is simply a matter of protecting the plant with cloches; parsley, for example, responds to this treatment. It is worth pointing out that all herbs will grow best in winter and come to less harm if they are on well-drained soil and in a sunny, well-sheltered position. In gardens where the soil and conditions vary considerably, it is worth setting aside an area for winter herbs. Parsley can also be grown in a cold frame. Some people simply lift the plants in early autumn and transplant these in the frame. As a rule this is a quicker method of supplying leaves than making a late sowing in the frame, but much depends upon the amount of space that is available.

Some other herbs can be lifted and these are usually transplanted into pots or boxes and grown on in more warmth than can be provided by a cold frame, in a greenhouse for example, or even indoors under lights. These include basil, fennel, mint and tarragon. Rosemary can be pot grown entirely, brought indoors and stood in good light, and taken out again in spring. This should be necessary only in cold regions because rosemary is hardy enough for most gardens so long as it is given a sunny and sheltered spot. It is also a good plant for the seaside.

Some herbs can be transplanted into boxes and moved indoors during the winter. To offset indoor gloom they can be placed under fluorescent lights.

The soil is usually moist in autumn and as a rule plants can be lifted easily enough, but should the season be dry, water the plants well for an hour or two before lifting so that the roots come up in a moist mass. Select a flower pot which will take the root ball comfortably. If necessary, place a little good soil at the bottom of the pot. The crown of the plant should be kept above soil level, just as it was when it grew in the garden, yet there should be a space left between the soil surface and the rim of the pot to take water. Fill any space between the root ball and the sides of the pot with good potting soil. Make sure that this is firm, as firm as the soil in the root ball. Pour in a little soil to begin with and then ram it down with the fingers or a stick. Add a little more and so on until the top level is reached. Water the plant in and let it drain. Leave it out of doors in a shady place for a few days to let it become settled in the pot before bringing it indoors. Spray the foliage over with clean water from time to time but do not keep the soil wet. Let this dry out a little so that the roots are activated into working properly to search for moisture. Do not let the soil become too dry, however. When you water next time, pour in the water so that the space between soil and pot rim is filled. The water should course through the soil.

Mint can be grown in a deep seed box. Almost fill this with soil. Spread the mint roots all over the surface, cover them with more soil and water them in well. Bring the box indoors. Incidentally, remember that mint will go on producing shoots well into early winter if you keep cutting the plants and prevent the stems running to flower.

As with all other herbs, it is more helpful to fill more than one box of mint so that boxes can be brought in in succession. If you grow mint in a pot on a sunny window-sill, keep it standing in a saucer of water. When growing mint in pots, see that one-third of the pot is filled with drainage material, e.g. shingle, pebbles, broken flower

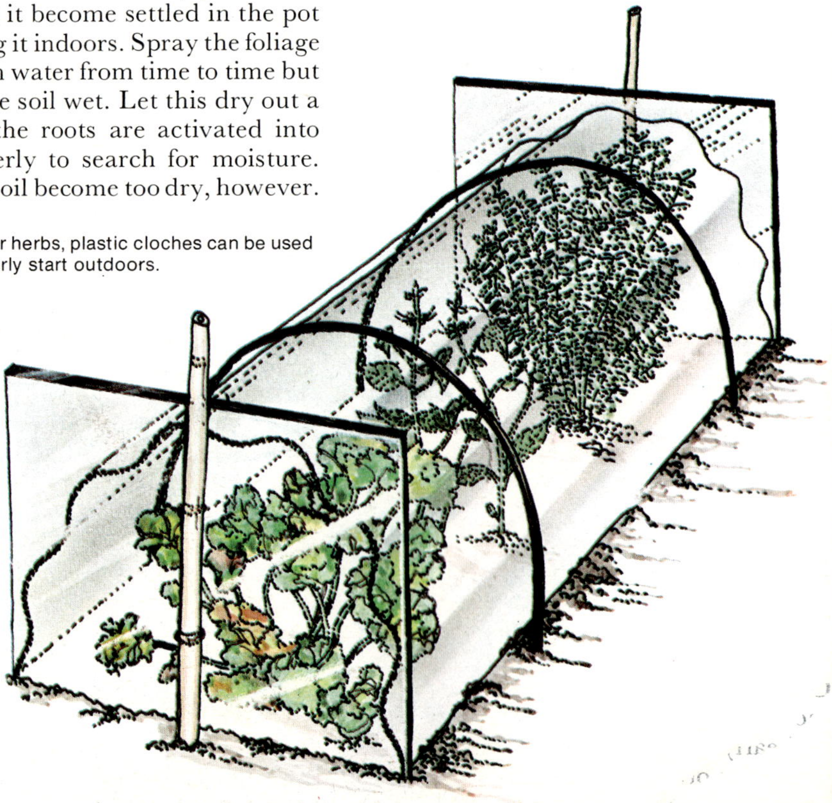

Though unusual for herbs, plastic cloches can be used to give them an early start outdoors.

Herbs raised indoors in pots must be given an adequate growing medium. Drainage material should be laid in the bottom of the pot. Bits of pebble and broken pot fragments, coarse gravel and charcoal pieces are all suitable for this purpose. They should be topped with a good potting compost in which the plants' roots can flourish and grow.

pots (remember, though, that clay pots are becoming rarer) and crushed brick, topped with a few nuggets of charcoal. This will ensure that the soil stays moist but does not become water-logged and sour.

If space is available, it is possible to raise a succession of batches of marjoram, basil and chives, simply by sowing a pinch in small pots, then snipping the entire growth off as soon as it is large enough to be of use. Onion seed can also be grown this way and the pungent 'grass' is excellent in winter and early spring salads.

It is important to understand that potted herbs are not house plants and will not tolerate the low light intensity indoors for long. Even a sunny windowsill does not give as well-lit a home as a place outdoors. If plants soon become drawn and spindly they are not getting enough light. Sometimes plant foods help to correct this weak growth a little. It helps to turn the container a quarter turn each day so that all parts of the plant face the light on a regular basis at some time.

It is also important that the air in which the plants are growing is unpolluted. Domestic gas and oil fumes both take their toll of many plants grown indoors and herbs are no exception.

7 *Cosmetic and potpourri herbs*

Borage (left), with its brilliant blue flowers, makes a refreshing hot or cold tea. Both its furry leaves and bright flowers are used for this purpose.

Honeysuckle (right) twines itself decoratively along walls, fences and arches. Its flowers add a delightful perfume to potpourris.

Lavender flowers (far right) are used to make scented water and lavender bags and to lend fragrance to potpourris. The flowers can also be candied.

Many herbs are grown for their sweetly scented leaves and flowers or even for their roots. From them are made potpourris, scented waters, scented sugars and other confections, tisanes or teas, conserves and syrups, shampoos and soaps, to mention only a few of the most important products. Besides adding to the spice of life, in more ways than one, these same plants add greatly to the interest, attraction and charm of a herb garden.

We have already seen that in some cases, such as with roses and lavenders, plants can be used as boundaries. Carnations and pinks can be prettily grouped among evergreen thymes in a border and since the grey-green foliage of these plants is handsome and also evergreen – although perhaps not so profuse in winter – the plants furnish a border for most of the year.

Hyssop will produce purple and pink flowers that look pretty among green parsley or feathery dill. Bergamot adds height as well as colour to a border.

Honeysuckle can be grown up poles, over archways or trained to cover a wall or a bank. Where there is space for climbers and the climate is mild, the sweetly scented jasmine, *Jasminum officinale* can be grown. The white flowers go in potpourri and they can be used for jasmine tea. The yellow winter jasmine is not scented.

In a well protected garden or in mild areas, the lemon-scented verbena, *Lippia citriodora,* deserves to be grown. This is a shrub which sometimes makes a small tree and is deciduous. The fragrance of the leaves is very strong. Another, smaller shrub, the sun rose, *Cistus ladaniferus,* which needs a sheltered place and light well drained soil, has aromatic leaves. So does the neat, shrubby St John's wort, *Hypericum patulum,* which smells of resin and tangerine when the leaves are bruised. Its handsome variety *Henryi* is also scented. Mock orange or *Philadelphus coronarius* and any of the other fragrant species of the same genera are ideal for scented gardens. If these are to be screened or divided from the rest, it is possible to make a border from scented

shrubs, including roses and lavender, thyme, rosemary and, of course, bay.

As one would expect, the roses used for potpourri and scented toilet waters or other items, should be highly scented. Usually, the red-petalled roses are most highly favoured since these usually have the sweetest perfume, sometimes with a hint of lemon in it, but this is not a hard and fast rule. Both modern and old-fashioned varieties and some species can be used. Among the most scented species are *Rosa centifolia*, the cabbage or Provence rose; *R. damascena*, the damask rose; *R. gallica officinalis*, the French rose; and all of the many varieties of moss roses.

It should be understood that these are not roses for small gardens. Often they are called 'shrub' roses because they are not pruned back hard each year like the modern hybrid teas and floribundas. In time each bush occupies an area of ground over half a metre square (several square feet). One should remember also that if the roses are to be gathered when they are at their

The pretty open flowers of the briar rose (left) can b trained as colourful hedges. Bright nasturtium flowe (below) also lend a lovely spicy taste to salads.

The delicate pink moss rose (above) has a ravishing scent. Though brief-flowering, it is ideal for potpourris.

best they will not add much to the colour in the garden.

The scented-leaved sweet briar, which has already been described, is sometimes sold under its synonym, *R. rubiginosa* instead of *R. eglanteria*. It has a double variety, *duplex*. Although the natural habit is t grow 150–200cm (5–7ft) tall, this ros makes a good low hedge if it is clipped bac each spring just before growth begins. I later, the leafy shoots are clipped for dry ing, this also tends to keep the plants nea and compact.

Of course, not all of the plants used fo potpourri, for liqueurs, for candying or fo any of the other uses, need be grown in a herb garden proper. Some can be set abou the garden as isolated plants – shrubs ar often best grown this way. Some can tak their place in the usual type of border o bed. Some can be used as ground covers This term is given to plants which grow sc thickly that in time they cover a large are of soil with a thick cover of foliage. Thi discourages the growth of weeds because i prevents their seeds from germinating freely. Ground covers also help to keep the soil moist round the base of shrubs and taller plants.

One of the best plants for this purpose is a little woodland plant, the woodruff or *Asperula odorata*. The scented dried flowers can also be used as a tea. They are sometimes mixed with China tea to make it go a

Recipe for a herb potpourri

Flowers	*Leaves (dried)*		*Spices*
borage	angelica	mint	cinnamon
camomile	basil	rosemary	cloves
elder	bay	sage	nutmeg
lavender	bergamot	sweet cicely	
marigold petals	borage	tarragon	
nasturtium	lemon balm		
rose petals	lovage		
violet	marjoram		

Place a selection of leaves, flowers and spices from the above lists in a wide bowl. Put them in layers, using the flowers which are the most attractive for the layer which is topmost (visible).

little further as well as to enhance its own fragrance.

Another good ground cover, with larger leaves than the woodruff, is *Geranium macrorrhizum*. Bruise the leaves, either by accident or on purpose, and their powdery fragrance fills the air. Thymes also can be used as carpeting plants, as we have already learned, but these need not necessarily spread themselves on stone or pathways. They will also help to clothe a bank.

Pinks are extremely hardy plants. They will grow in ordinary soil and will flower freely so long as this is rich. Prepare the soil well before planting and feed the plants with a liquid plant food in spring and autumn. Pinks like the sun. They can be grown in beds where their attractive grey-green tufted shoots will soon smother the ground. They also look good grown in a

Choose the ingredients for a potpourri with care. A well-made one will remain scented for years.

wide band to edge a path. And they also look attractive this way sprawled out before lavender. They will even carpet the ground below apple trees or some similar plants; so long as they are not in deep shade a little partial shade during the day will do them no harm.

There are annual, biennial and perennial kinds of pinks, but naturally, those with the most petals are the best for potpourri. There are some highly scented double varieties of *Dianthus plumarius*, some of which possess a strong clove fragrance. Consult catalogues for varieties and descriptions.

It is possible to make an attractive border of all scented plants, concentrating on those whose flowers are used, but alternating them with some of the more attractive of the scented-leaved kinds. Fortunately, many of these are a soft grey-green and so are the perfect foil and buffer alike for any vividly coloured blooms near them.

A few members of the daisy family can be grown. Costmary, *Chrysanthemum balsamita*, has attractive grey-green leaves, and tiny yellow button-like flowers borne in clusters on straight stems. Camomile, besides being used for tea, can add to the attractive ppearance of potpourri and contribute a ittle of its own particular scent into the bargain. The dried petals of the pot narigold, *Calendula officinalis*, also add colour and pungency to potpourri.

A few sage leaves can be used in flower nixtures and more of the sages can be grown to provide colour. The annual clary, *alvia sclarea*, nowadays comes in several prettily coloured varieties, whose bracts lecorating the stem ends are ruby, magenta, purple and violet. These give more colour than scent to potpourri, but like some other herbs, their scent is stronger when the lowers are dried.

Artemisias – of which family tarragon is he best known herb, although some of the others are used in the preparation of iqueurs – are more scented than pungent. These include lad's love or southernwood, nentioned earlier. *A. absinthium* is common vormwood, *A. vulgaris* is mugwort, *A. pontica* is Roman wormwood, *A. tridentata* is the sage bush (a confusing name since this is not a sage). This species grows really tall, 2–2·5m (6–8ft), and is silvery and fragrant.

All parts of the handsome angelica – roots, stems and leaves – are fragrant. Besides being used for confectionery, it plays an important role in potpourri. The roots should be cleaned, dried and powdered for culinary use.

Other culinary herbs which are used in potpourris are marjoram, balm, mints and borage. The latter is used for the flower's colour, not perfume, and marjoram, balm and mints can be candied.

Of the annuals, possibly mignonette is the most delightfully scented. Where there is little garden space for it, the plant will grow well in all kinds of containers outdoors and as a pot plant in a greenhouse or on a sunny windowsill. Wallflowers are often overlooked, yet these are an excellent way of adding colour to the herb garden in the spring, so long as one takes care to see that they do not smother the perennial herbs. They also grow well in tubs and other containers. They could occupy the area set aside for herbs that will be planted out in late spring, basil for example. When the wallflowers are pulled up after flowering, enrich the soil with a little plant food.

Vivid floral arrangements can be made from herbs. Roses, camomile, borage and calendula (pot marigold) spill colourfully from a vase (left). Wallflowers (right) are a vibrantly colourful addition to any herb garden. Purple-leaved basil (below) is an ornamental variety well suited to herb borders.

8 Drying herbs

Obviously, all the herbs used in potpourris dry well and the same methods are used for these as for the culinary kinds. Some of the latter dry much better than others. Generally speaking it is the shrubby labiates, the kinds with lipped flowers, which dry best – sage, thyme, marjoram and rosemary for instance. These all retain their essential oils and are strongly flavoured even when dry or powdered. The same is true of bay. Some of the soft-leaved kinds dry well enough but are likely to be disappointing when used, parsley and mint being examples. Chives, balm, borage, chervil and fennel are really not worth drying. Fortunately these are available – or can be made so – in winter and the cook does not have to depend upon dried supplies.

Usually just the tips of stems are taken. They should be cut and not picked or pulled, so that they come away cleanly from the plant with no faded stem ends, or portions of root with soil still clinging to them. By picking the tips the plant is encouraged to make more growth. The time to gather herbs is when the plants are ready to come into flower, for it is at this time that their flavours are strongest. However, this is not a hard and fast rule, and many people harvest the herbs two or three times a year.

If many herbs are to be dried, it is best to make the shoots into small bunches of one kind so that once these are hung up, the air can circulate round each shoot.

There are various methods of drying the bunches. If the weather is warm they can be dried by hanging them upside down outdoors in the shade. They should not be put out until the warmest, dryest part of the day and they should not be left outside overnight in case of heavy dews moistening them again. They should not, of course, be hung in any place where they are likely to become dusty.

If there is no suitable place outdoors, or in damp weather, the bunches can be hung indoors in a warm kitchen, away from steam, or in an airing cupboard.

If only small amounts are to be dried, the simplest method is to spread them out on paper or on a sieve and turn them from time to time so that all parts are exposed to the air. Another easy way to dry small quantities is to place them, in their individual kinds, in small net bags and then to hang these in some dry, clean and airy place. Herbs simply laid on a sunny windowsill indoors will dry very quickly, but one should bear in mind that those which are dried away from sunlight keep their colour best. Also, the faster herbs dry, the better their colour.

When herbs are dusty, or thought to be so, make them into bunches, draw them through clean water agitating them so that any dust is removed and then shake or

Herbs can be dried in a warm kitchen by hanging them in small bunches before grinding them fine for cooking.

swish them in the air until all the surplus moisture is thrown off. After this, make them into smaller bunches or spread them out, depending upon what method is used to dry them.

Take care when using an oven to dry herbs, because too much heat dries out the essential oils. Some people spread the dried herbs on oven foil or baking sheets and dry them a further ten minutes in a preheated oven at 200°F/gas 1. This might be a prudent move in a damp season, but usually it is possible to tell by touch whether or not the herbs are dry enough.

It is possible from this point to store them as they are in their bunches. They can, for instance, be enclosed in a paper or plastic bag to keep them dust-free. Alternatively, they can be cleaned from their stalks and stored in air-tight jars. Some can be mixed and put into small muslin or cheesecloth squares to make a bouquet garni. The dry leaves are easily stripped from their stalks; let them fall on to clean paper and then lightly rub them between the hands to reduce them to crumbs. To make a really fine powder, bay leaf powder for instance, grind the herbs in an electric grinder. Traces of herb flavour can be removed by wiping the grinder round with lemon juice.

Potpourri petals and leaves are not usually rubbed or crumbled. Incidentally, one of the best and least troublesome ways of drying petals is to use the string bag method. Pack the petals in loosely and use a large mesh netting. When the petals seem dry, spread them out in some airy place indoors to let them finish off.

If cut herbs are to be kept for a day or two it is best to treat them as cut flowers and to stand them in water out of direct sunshine. If they are to be kept in a refrigerator, store them in an airtight container but not too near the freezer compartment.

Herbs will deep-freeze but the longer they are left frozen, the more will they lose their flavour. (There really is nothing so good as growing fresh supplies the year round.) Chives will not keep their texture or their flavour, yet vichyssoise soup flavoured with chives will freeze well. This soup should of course have the chives added at the last moment.

Mint is best made into mint sauce and frozen in small quantities.

Parsley should not be chopped if it is to be deep-frozen or it will lose most of its flavour. Wash and dry the sprigs after the main stem has been cut off. Press these down into a container and freeze. When ready to use, in soups or sauces and not as a garnish, turn out the complete block and either grate or shave it.

A good way to store mixed dried herbs so that they are conveniently assembled and ready to use is to make them into a wrapped bouquet garni, briefly referred to earlier. The basic herbs which should always be included are parsley, thyme and bay although stronger and more aromatic herbs are often needed, especially for marinades. It is a good plan to prepare a few bouquets for special dishes in which different herbs are allowed to predominate. Thus, for boiling fowls or chicken the bouquets should be mostly tarragon whereas for beef stews extra marjoram should be included. For a court-bouillon (fish stock), one could make a bouquet that includes parsley roots, celery, fennel, thyme, bay, coriander seeds and a few pepper corns.

Herbs make attractive gifts when wrapped as bouquets. These can be packed into air-tight glass jars so that they will not lose their flavour quite so rapidly. If you are certain that the recipient will be quick to store the herbs, you could even assemble them in a Cordon Bleu garland. Begin by preparing the little bouquet bags. First, cut three or four-inch squares of muslin and have ready several lengths of fine twine. For a small bouquet garni use a level teaspoonful of the mixed, crushed herbs. Gather up the four corners and tie the little bundle lightly using the twine, leaving a long end so that the bag can easily be pulled out.

A Cordon Bleu garland (above) is a splendid wreath of intertwined herb sachets, shallots and bay leaves.

Dried herbs (left) must be stored in air-tight jars.

Take a strip of plastic-covered wire netting, roll it up and shape it into a circle. Cover this with blue crepe paper. Transform the bouquet garni bags into 'apples' by pushing a clove into the centre of each. Back each 'apple' with two bay leaves. You can join these with some wire-spined twists used to close bags. Use the thread on the muslin bag to fasten the bay leaves to the 'apple' and to tie the entire bunch to a cocktail stick. Push the stick down through the plastic covered wire netting. Alternate the 'apples' with shallots, also mounted on false cocktail stick stems.

9 Wild herbs

Some of our garden herbs have been lomesticated from the wild. Others have scaped from cultivation and become native. Nowadays, most of the wild herbs hat are gathered are used to make wines and preserves although some still continue o be valued for their old uses. One of these s the elder blossom. The dried blossoms can be added to tea, to gooseberry jams and o pies and dishes of all kinds. They can also be pounded into lard to make a soothing ointment for burns and can be mixed with lried peppermint to make a tisane against nfluenza. Freshly picked, elder blossoms can be dipped in batter and fried then lrained, sugared and eaten as a dessert. The fragrant flowers of broom also make a good wine and the buds can be pickled as false capers. Dandelion leaves are good in salads and their flowers make a delicious wine as do those of white clover. Red clover can be made into a tea to ease whooping cough. The small white flowers of feverfew, make a tonic tea. Wild thyme, marjoram and mints can be used to flavour meat dishes. They can also be blended into potpourris along with lime flowers, meadowsweet, camomile, hawthorn, meliot, sweet cicely, sweet flag leaves, tansy, woodruff and others.

Hundreds of different varieties of wild rose (above) brighten countryside fields. The leaves of dandelions (left), one of the most common of herbs, make delicious salads and teas. The delicate white-flowered elder (below left) grows wild in hedges and fields. Elder blossoms make a refreshing tea.

10 Uses of herbs

To many people, herbs are simply plants which are used, usually in a dried state, to flavour meats and stuffings or to give zest to soups or sauces. Yet herbs can play a much more important role than this. Before the introduction of modern chemical drugs, herbs were the source of a wide array of medicines, salves and ointments of all kinds. The word 'drug' comes from the Anglo-Saxon 'drigan' – to dry – and is a reference to the manner in which medicinal plants were preserved for use.

In former times, such plants, most of which are now neglected, were grown in special plots or were gathered in fields or forests. People believed that there was always a plant somewhere which could be used to cure, or at least counteract, the ill effects of every disease or pain.

It seems that some plants were chosen simply because they appeared to have some obvious affinity with a disease. Thus, the bright, yellow-flowered greater celandine with its acrid juice was considered a herb to be used against jaundice. Herbs were also widely used to staunch wounds and to knit broken bones as well as to make fomentations and poultices for swellings and for wounds that had turned septic. The pretty little centaury is said to have been so named because a Greek centaur used the plant to heal the wounds made by a poisoned arrow.

White wine vinegar can be given a delicious and subtle herbal flavour by allowing sprigs of thyme to marinate in it.

To this day, many herbs are still used as a prophylactic against colds or as a febrifuge. Others are to be recommended as gargles for sore throats.

A great many herbs, particularly the

Herb teas (above) are some of the most refreshing hot drinks. They are renowned for their restorative and soothing properties. Tarragon (right) will impart a delicate flavour to olive oil.

aromatic artemisia group (such as mugwort and wormwood), are used to flavour liqueurs. Juniper berries are also used to flavour gin and like so many other herbs also are used in cooking, especially to flavour sauerkraut and many meat dishes, such as veal. Sorrel was highly valued in the days when only salt-preserved meat was available in the depths of winter because it is a natural tenderiser. Leaves wrapped round a joint before it is cooked render the meat more palatable.

Few people consider Indian or China tea to be made from a herb yet the *Camellia sinensis* leaves which are infused or brewed are but one of the many different kinds of teas or tisanes made from the leaves or flowers of plants. In many countries teas are also made from plants other than the camellia. For instance, in North America a brew made from bergamot is known as Oswego tea. Most teas are intended as refreshing drinks, but some are particularly noted for their medicinal and soothing qualities. Most are brewed in the same manner as ordinary tea and are taken either hot or cold with perhaps a little sugar or honey. Camomile is a very popular tea and is deliciously fragrant. Woodruff tea, although it can be drunk on its own, is also blended with Indian or China teas to make these go a little further and to enhance their flavours. At one time mugwort, *Artemisia vulgaris,* was used as a tea substitute even though its original use was in the brewing of beers. Lime-flower tea is considered by some people to be the most refreshing of all.

In the past, many more herbs were used in salads than are today, and this included the flowers as well as the leaves, as the vegetables we now know as salad were not so intensively cultivated then. The memory lingers on, however, in the name of Salad Burnet, a plant which has a hint of cucumber in its scent and is still to be recommended for salads.

Savoury dishes

ANGELICA
Angelica archangelica

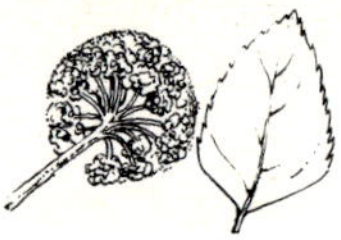

In salads, use raw stems and thick leaf midribs.

BALM, LEMON BALM
Melissa officinalis

Use chopped finely in sauces and salads, in stuffings or forcemeats for veal and poultry.

BASIL
Ocimum basilicum and
O. minimum

Use fresh or dried with tomatoes, white fish, ham and in many Italian dishes. Makes a splendid garnish for beans of all kinds, squash, courgettes and other marrows.

BAY
Laurus nobilis

Essential in bouquets garnis. Use fresh or dried to flavour savoury dishes. (Dried leaves can be ground to a powder, which should always be stored in an air-tight container.)

BERGAMOT, OSWEGO TEA
Monarda didyma

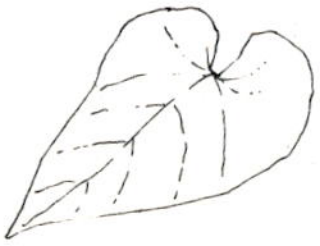

Use fresh leaves and flowers in salads, but in moderation because of their pungency.

BORAGE
Borago officinalis

Use very young leaves in salads.

CAMOMILE
Anthemis nobilis

CARAWAY
Carum carvi

The leaves and stems are not eaten. The seeds are used as a spice.

CHERVIL
Anthriscus cerefolium

As an essential ingredient of *fines herbes*, with parsley and tarragon, it is used in omelettes and other egg dishes, salads and salad dressings, poultry and some white fish. Use as a delicate garnish for vegetable purées, or with shell fish and with cream soups.

CHIVES
Allium schoenoprasum

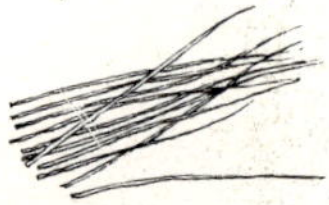

Cook only by adding to a dish at the last moment or as a garnish or condiment. Cut 'grass' finely with scissors. Blend with butter for garnishing grilled meats and fish.

Sweet dishes	Drinks	Potpourris, etc.	Other uses
Cook stalks as a sweet or as a conserve mixed with rhubarb. Candy them for confectionery.	Use leaves as a tisane. Use roots in liqueurs.	Dry roots for potpourri.	
		Dry and mix in potpourri.	
Use fresh or dried in milk puddings.		Mix leaves or powder in potpourri.	
	Use fresh or dried as a tisane or mix dried leaves with Indian tea to make it go further and add to its flavour.	Mix dried flowers and leaves in potpourri.	
Cook young leaves in batter, with the flowers, as fritters. Flowers can also be candied.	Add sprigs of fresh flowers and leaves to fruit cups and iced drinks.	Use dried flowers for colour in potpourri.	
	Main use, fresh or dry as a soothing tisane. Gather daisy heads when the outer ray petals begin to turn back but while centres are still bright.	Mix dried flowers in potpourri.	Boil flowers in rain water as a hair rinse for blondes.
The leaves and stems are not eaten. The seeds are used as a flavouring in confectionery.			

Savoury dishes

CORIANDER
Coriandrum sativum

The aromatic seeds are used as flavouring, and are an important ingredient in curries. Coriander is always included in mixed spice.

CUMIN
Cuminum cyminum

Use as a spice in curries and in sauces for fish.

DILL
Peucedanum graveolens

Cook young shoots, like mint, with new potatoes and add moderately to potato dishes. Garnish peas with the finely chopped leaves. Excellent with cucumber. Use flower heads and seeds to flavour cucumber pickles. Use seeds (very pungent) in heavy white sauces.

FENNEL
Foeniculum vulgare

Cook young leaves or shoots with fish, veal and offal. Use raw with tinned fish, chopped finely like parsley. Blend in curries. Seeds are very pungent and good in sauces and fish mousse. Fennel dries well, but becomes strongly flavoured and must be used with care.

GARLIC
Allium sativum

An essential ingredient in many dishes. The individual bulbs, known as 'cloves', are either crushed or chopped. Leaves can also be used.

LAVENDER
Lavendula officinalis

Not often used in cooking, but can be used like rosemary with poultry.

LOVAGE
Ligusticum officinale

Good substitute for celery flavour. Use stem in stocks and bouillon. Use young leaves, ribs and stems finely sliced in salads or soups. Use moderately when dried.

MARIGOLD
Calendula officinalis

Pot marigold can be used to flavour soups and also to make an attractive garnish for a salad. Fresh or dried petals can be used.

MARJORAM
Origanum dictamnus,
O. marjorana,
O. onites

An essential bouquet garni herb for marinades. Use sweet or knotted marjoram in casseroles, stews, soups and terrines. Dries well, but use discreetly. Suits lamb, pork and beef. Pot marjoram is best for salads and egg dishes. Mix with thyme and parsley for scrambled eggs and omelettes.

MINT
Mentha piperita,
M. pulegium
M. rotundifolia,
M. spicata

Cook pennyroyal with new potatoes, spearmint with peas. The round,woolly-leaved apple mint is best for mint sauce. Mint leaves can be used in salads and sauces, or chopped and sprinkled on lamb and mutton for roasts. Does not dry well because aroma becomes too strong.

weet dishes	Drinks	Potpourris, etc.	Other uses
oriander is used in weets and for flavouring quor, especially gin.			
			Use in veterinary medicine as a carminative.
se the seeds, which are ery pungent, like araway, to flavour bread nd cakes.			
prigs in a jar of sugar will cent and flavour it.		Used mainly in toilet waters, sweet-smelling bags and potpourri.	
eeds are used in onfectionery.			
Can be used to flavour custards.		Pot marigold is best known as an ingredient of potpourri.	
		Mix dried leaves and flowers in potpourri.	
Use mint leaves in sorbets. Leaves can be crystallised.	Use mint leaves in iced drinks, fruit cups and tisanes.	Use pineapple mint leaves in potpourri.	

Savoury dishes

NASTURTIUM
Tropaeolum majus

Once known as Indian Cress because of the cress-like taste of its flowers, leaves and seeds. All can be used in salads, and the seeds can be used as a substitute for horse radish.

PARSLEY
Petroselinum crispum

An essential bouquet garni herb. Very versatile: seems to suit eggs, all meats and fish. Used widely as a garnish. Can be fried and used this way. As a condiment, chop finely and add to the dish at the last moment to keep the colour bright. Best used fresh, but will dry.

POPPY
Papaver somniferum

ROSEMARY
Rosmarinus officinalis

Good cooked with all meats and poultry. Chop finely and sprinkle on roasts. Mix with chopped garlic for lamb and kid. Use sprig to flavour pea, pulse, spinach and minestrone soups and add to old boiled potatoes. Will dry, but becomes very pungent.

SAGE
Salvia officinalis

One of the most popular of herbs, in its dried form it is used mostly in stuffing or forcemeat. Good fresh and well chopped – in cream and cottage cheese or sprinkled on meats to be roasted or grilled.

SAVORY, WINTER AND SUMMER
Satureia hortensis,
S. montana

Summer savory considered to have the finer flavour of the two, similar to thyme. Excellent in forcemeats for goose, turkey, chicken, veal and pork. Mix with chives and parsley for duck. Use for trout and other freshwater fish. Include in bouquet garni for all marinades and when poaching fish. Cook with broad beans and peas.

SHALLOT
Allium ascalonicum

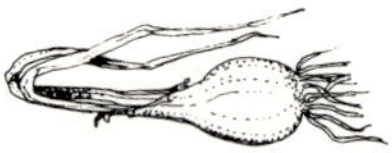

Has a distinct flavour midway between garlic and onion. Can be used young or allowed to ripen and be stored for winter use. Leaves can be used like chives.

TARRAGON
Artemisia dracunculus

An essential ingredient of *fines herbes*. Cook with chicken boiled or roasted. Use for stuffing and pâte, white fish, rabbit, veal and all egg dishes. Used in hollandaise, béarnaise and tartare sauces. Serve in tarragon butter with shell fish. Dries well, but becomes very pungent.

THYME
Thymus vulgaris,
T x citriodorus

Common thyme is an essential bouquet garni herb. Very pungent when fresh, so use discreetly. Use with all kinds of meats, poultry, fish, soups, forcemeats, marinades. Use in onion, marrow family, aubergine and salsify dishes. Add lemon thyme to any savoury dish for a slight lemon flavour. Blend with butter for grills.

WOODRUFF
Asperula odorata

·weet dishes	Drinks	Potpourris, etc.	Other uses
·he dark grey oily seeds ·e used in confectionery.			The seeds are used in bread-making.
·lowers can be candied.	Makes a good tisane, fresh or dried.		When boiled in water resulting liquid makes excellent hair rinse.
·Jse lemon thyme in milk ·uddings.		Mix dried thymes of any species in potpourri.	
	Can be used as a tisane or tea. It is often blended with fine teas – China or Indian – to make them go further and to enhance their flavour.	Can be used as an ingredient in potpourri or alone in scent bags to be laid among linen.	

Index